A compelling collection exploring the complexity and beauty of identity, motherhood, and faith. Nancy Heiss is an insightful and essential new voice in Mormon poetry.

—Katherine Cowley
winner of the 2018 Mormon Lit Blitz and
author of *The Secret Life of Miss Mary Bennet*

Reading these poems was an experience both poignant and deeply relatable. Heiss's ability to write in a way that is down-to-earth while also exploring powerful universal themes and emotions makes her words something to cherish and read again and again.

—Shallee McArthur
author of *The Unhappening of Genesis Lee*

PARADOXICAL * GLORY

BY COMMON CONSENT PRESS is a non-profit publisher dedicated to producing affordable, high-quality books that help define and shape the Latter-day Saint experience. BCC Press publishes books that address all aspects of Mormon life. Our mission includes finding manuscripts that will contribute to the lives of thoughtful Latter-day Saints, mentoring authors and nurturing projects to completion, and distributing important books to the Mormon audience at the lowest possible cost.

WITH ART FROM

BROOKE NEWHART

BCC PRESS

Paradoxical Glory
Copyright © 2022 by Nancy Heiss

All rights reserved. Printed in the United States of America. No part of this book may be used or reproduced in any manner whatsoever without written permission except in the case of brief quotations embodied in critical articles or reviews.

For information contact
By Common Consent Press
4900 Penrose Dr.
Newburgh, IN 47630

Cover photograph: LL Ori and the Orion Nebula; NASA, ESA and the Hubble Heritage Team
Cover design: Brooke Newhart with D Christian Harrison
Book design: Andrew Heiss

www.bccpress.org
ISBN-13: 978-1-948218-40-5

10 9 8 7 6 5 4 3 2 1

Nancy:
To my children, who give me so much writing fodder,
to Andrew, who believed that I could,
and to my mom, who always knew I would.

Brooke:
To my parents, for their
eternal support and loving kindness

CONTENTS

Introduction	1
The syndrome	5
Ideas vs. the world	6
Looking down	8
Something extraordinary	10
How great shall be your joy	13
Preferences	13
A proclamation	13
Mother-in-waiting	14
Feminists are mothers, too	17
Runner up I	20
Childlike faith	21
The woman behind the curtain	22
Help thou mine unbelief	26
With child	27
Is it I?	28
Trophy wife	29
The last weaning	31
Beauty for ashes	32
Give them a name	34
To Sampson	35

And a blessing	36
Redacted	36
Victim of fertility	38
My box of chocolates	40
Remembrance	41
Mommy brainstorming	41
Mythos	42
Runner up II	45
The birth story	45
Postpartum depression	47
Peace by piece	48
Just right	50
Be ye therefore perfect	52
Come unto me	53
Little fish	54
In my mother's arms	55
I Am	56
A child's prayer	58
The last baby	58
The door	60
SOS	61
Milk music	64
Lactational amenorrhea	64
Midnight feedings and family planning	65
Bombs away	66
I once was blind	66

BRCA	69
Russian superstitions	71
Accidental cat lady	72
Collections	73
Souvenir	74
Rain shadow	75
I watched my mother grow up	77
There shall be a record kept among you	78
Finding my voice	79
Love letters	82
A first date	83
The dream catcher	84
Old wives tales	86
Not good enough	88
Mop, mop, mop	89
Chore charts	90
Role reversal	90
Gender roles	91
Rented spaces	92
Baptist testimony	93
Moving on	94
Settling in	96
My frail existence	98
My thoughts ≠ Your thoughts	99
I don't want this sadness	101
They came running	102

Burnt offerings	104
Object permanence	107
Cookies for the sad	108
Crushed velvet	108
A chiasmus	109
A bedtime prayer	110
Pen pals	110
Miriam's worry (and the answer)	111
The infinity scarf	112
A well-intended lady	114
Deconstruction	115
Food storage	118
Four-generation honey	119
Phantom pains	120
I see dead people	121
The first holiday without you	121
Missing mother	123
Finding mother	124
Christmas yet to come	126
We, the rising generation	127
Wither and bloom	128
Notes	131

INTRODUCTION

These poems came to me in a season of grief. I was mourning so many losses, so many changes, so many partings, and I felt very uprooted. Among other challenges, our family made two back-to-back cross-country moves, my mother-in-law (one of my biggest supporters and best friends) passed away, and, with the birth of my last baby, I suffered a mid-mom crisis.

I knew from a very young age that I wanted to be a mother, and when the opportunity came, I welcomed the experience with all my heart. I thought it would bring me indescribable joy. And it did!

But motherhood is not a light packer.

Along with joy, motherhood brought a whole lot of other baggage—anxiety, depression, and the realization that motherhood, however wonderful, isn't as fulfilling as I imagined it would be. Having these tiny humans completely dependent on me gave me a sense of purpose—the almost overwhelming directive to tend these souls, fresh from heaven. It was a job I threw myself into completely. I didn't have to think about myself when every minute of every day was consumed by my children and, as overwhelming as it was, I loved it. But soon I came to realize I was working myself out of a job.

Each exciting achievement my children experienced tore a hole in my identity. Days that had once been filled dressing children, pushing swings, and reading stories began to feel empty—my children were growing up. As I held my last newborn baby in my arms, I realized that never again would anyone need me like he needed me in that moment. I didn't know what I would do when I wasn't needed like that anymore. I didn't know that my nest would begin to feel empty so early. I hadn't realized that motherhood was never meant to be my entire identity. I didn't anticipate feeling so lost.

So, I began to search for an identity, a purpose beyond motherhood. It hasn't been an easy quest. I have been told to simply "embrace my role as mother," a remark which stung because I *had* embraced that role, yet it was abandoning me. I was told that reaching beyond motherhood was "sinfully selfish," that I should be content with what I had. I wasn't sure that was possible because I've watched women sink into depression as their children left home, unable to fill the hole left behind. I've known women who have grown weary or bored with motherhood and have watched as their zest for life withers away. I have seen women turn to self-destructive or family-destructive behaviors to deal with their feelings of isolation and uselessness.

I was always taught that as people we are meant to act, not merely be acted upon,[1] so it didn't make sense to me that I should simply learn to be content with my life—with motherhood—as it is. Too often women are positioned in reactionary roles where their purpose is to respond to the cues of their

---

1. 2 Nephi 2:26

husband, their children, or their calling. While indeed laudable, I could not believe that this was everything I was meant to do. Our Heavenly Parents intend for us to be anxiously engaged[2] in life, which, for me, meant taking some initiative. I needed to act. I knew I needed to create, to be, to do—and not only support others in creating, being and doing—but I didn't know what that might look like for me.

Piling on to the dreadful feelings of watching my last baby grow up, I was then faced with the sudden loss of my mother-in-law and moving my family thousands of miles away from everything they knew. It was so overwhelming that I found myself at a loss for words. I could hardly string a sentence together, which was a strange feeling for me because as early as I knew I wanted to be a mother, I knew that I was a writer. I had always written—quietly—for myself, but suddenly I couldn't. Everything felt like too much; it was too big to write down. So, I stopped trying to force my big ideas onto a page and clung to the tiniest of phrases that would come to me in the middle of the night.

The poems that started this project, chronologically speaking, were BRCA, Midnight Feedings and Family Planning, and The Syndrome. Each one is so tiny, yet these small ideas opened the door for more and more words. So, I'd like to thank these poems for giving me my words back, for lending me space to explore my role and purpose, and for opening

---

2. D&C 58:27

the door for a conversation on motherhood that might help empower women to thrive beyond motherhood rather than shaming them for wanting anything more.

Mostly I'd like to thank you for reading my words, though if I may, I will offer this warning . . .

THE SYNDROME

I'm not a poet
I'm an imposter

IDEAS VS. THE WORLD

I shared my idea with the world.

The world said:
You can't do this.
Preposterous.
Sit down.

The idea said:
Keep trying.

Nancy Heiss

LOOKING DOWN

All around me
People were looking up
At the majesty
Of the pyramids.

But at the base of Khufu,
In the Saharan sand,
Lay a vixen.
Stiff.
Dead.
Ignored.
A mother,
Her teats swollen
With milk her kits would never drink.

I mourned for her, and,
With my own gurgling babe
Strapped to my chest,
Also swollen with milk,
I mourned for her babies
Pining away in their den,
Crying for their mother.

All around me
People were looking up
While someone's world had ended
Under their very noses.

Nancy Heiss

Woe unto them that are with child,
and to them that give suck in those days!
They have so much more to lose,
So much more to worry about!

But no one seemed to notice;
All around me
People were looking up.

Up is the apex of a pyramid.
Up is majestic and celestial.
Up is redemption, a pillar of light,
A serpent of brass put upon a pole.
Up is the Mountain of the Lord,
Moroni sounding his trumpet.

Down is the pit of despair.
Down is the lone and dreary world.
Down is trials and tribulation.
A certain man travelling from
   Jerusalem to Jericho.
Down is where Jesus stooped to
   write on the ground,
A lifeless fox on the desert sand.

Up is where we find God, but
Down is where we do God's work.

So, look up, yes.
But, oh, look down.

SOMETHING EXTRAORDINARY

We expect extraordinary occasions
And pressing calls—

> Relief Society Birthday Party!
> Relief Society Game Night!

We design to act in the name of the Lord—
to relieve the wants of the distressed,
and do all the good we can—

> Relief Society Craft-stravaganza!
> Relief Society Spa Day! Treat Yo Self!

As daughters of Zion, we should set an example
for all the world, rather than confine ourselves
to the course which had been heretofore pursued—

> Relief Society Chocolate Challenge!
> Relief Society Christmas Dinner!

Something's missing.

Something . . .

. . . extraordinary.

Nancy Heiss

HOW GREAT SHALL BE YOUR JOY

What if the one soul you can really bring to God
Is your own?

PREFERENCES

My children taught me:

There are things I want the
Father to do.

There are things I need
To struggle through.

There are things I want the
Mother to do.

A PROCLAMATION

Heavenly Mother is
Primarily responsible
For the nurture
Of her children.

Paradoxical Glory

MOTHER-IN-WAITING

I will always be a mother.
From the moment that first precious baby
Was placed in my arms—no. Before that.
I was a mother before that.

From the minute I felt those first
Popcorn-popping kicks—no. Before that.
I was a mother before that.

From the minute I heard the galloping
Of that tiny heartbeat—no. Before that.
I was a mother before that.

From the minute I saw that second line
Appear on the pregnancy test—no. Before that.
I was a mother before that.

From the very moment
Two worlds collided within me.
That is when I became a mother.

But, no. I was a mother before that, too.

I have always been a mother-in-waiting.

Nancy Heiss

My body, like a well-stocked refrigerator,
Possessed, from birth, an ample supply of eggs,
The possibility to flow with milk and honey.

My body, constantly preparing for motherhood,
Building nest after nest after nest after nest,
Eager for a universe to be planted inside.

My body, creating worlds without number,
A tribute to those that created me,
A vessel for those I create and all their potential.

My body, poised to juggle all at once the DNA
Of mother and father—of self and of lover—
Piecing together a puzzle—a child.

My body—essential to The Plan.
My motherhood—one eternal round.

Paradoxical Glory

FEMINISTS ARE MOTHERS, TOO

She scolded me:
You need to learn to embrace your role as mother.

Oh?

I yearned for child after child
Until they numbered a handful.
Each one took my breath away
And filled my heart to capacity.
But each time I found a way to love again—
Fiercely, passionately, unfathomably—
The slimy, squalling alien creature
Plopped into my exhausted arms,
Who only minutes before threatened
To split my whole being in twain.

Oh?

I spent a solid decade of my life
Breastfeeding. On. Demand.

Engorged,
With plugged ducts or
Full-blown mastitis,
I was fodder for new teeth.

Cracked nipples.
Nursing strikes.
Cluster feeds.

Midnight . . . 2 AM . . . 4 AM.

Pumping.
Pumping.
Pumping.

Milky comas.
Milky smiles.
Milky dribbles,

Cuddles, snuggles.
Endlessly staring into each other's eyes,
Falling desperately, easily in love.

Oh?

I have cheered each wibbly, wobbly step.
I have read that favourite story a million times.
I have checked over math homework and edited that essay.
I have hosted FHE and held nightly scripture study.
I have run preschool co-ops, volunteered in classrooms,
   and homeschooled.
I have cheered at soccer games and clapped at concerts.
I have baked birthday cakes and thrown birthday parties.
I have plied them with bandaids and tylenol.
I have prepared countless home cooked meals.
I have rushed them to the ER in the middle of the night.
I have combed their hair and brushed their teeth.
I have sung them lullabies and rubbed their backs.
I have squished a week's worth of stool looking for
   swallowed pennies.

Nancy Heiss

I have taught them how to read, to swim, to pray, to ride a bike,
To play the piano, and hopefully to be a decent person.

Oh?

I wouldn't say I've loved every minute,
But I've loved a good portion of it.
So, achievement unlocked:

Motherhood embraced.

What's next?

RUNNER UP I

She told me:
You are the best mom
In the whole entire . . .

. . . Neighbourhood.

Just in the neighbourhood?
Not in the world?

Not in the world, no.
There's got to be someone
better than you out there.

Oh, there is.

Nancy Heiss

CHILDLIKE FAITH

"Do you think fairies are real?"
She asked her brother.

"Oh, absolutely," he said.

"Do you think fairies are real?"
She asked her mother.

"Don't ask her," her brother said.
"Grown-ups are really bad at knowing
This sort of thing."

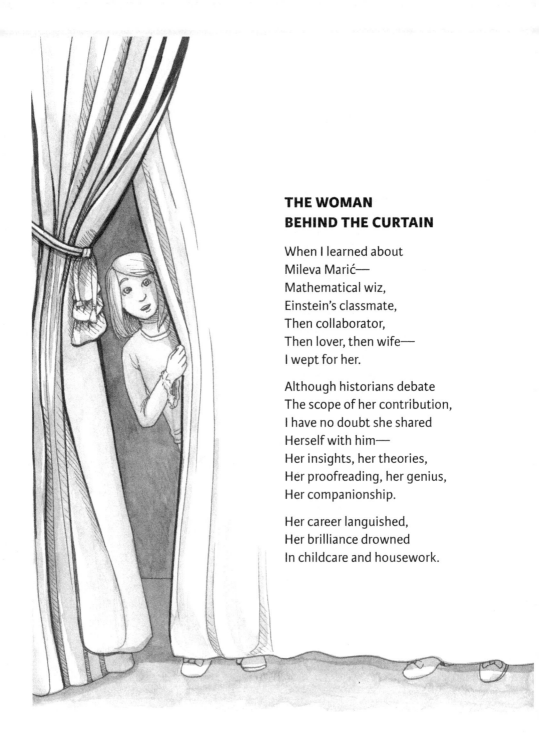

THE WOMAN BEHIND THE CURTAIN

When I learned about
Mileva Marić—
Mathematical wiz,
Einstein's classmate,
Then collaborator,
Then lover, then wife—
I wept for her.

Although historians debate
The scope of her contribution,
I have no doubt she shared
Herself with him—
Her insights, her theories,
Her proofreading, her genius,
Her companionship.

Her career languished,
Her brilliance drowned
In childcare and housework.

Nancy Heiss

Meanwhile, he claimed
General relativity
Special relativity
Photoelectric effect
(And a Nobel Prize).

He left Germany, Mileva, his sons,
And immigrated to America
With his new wife—his cousin—
And became hopelessly famous.

When I ache for Mileva,
I ache for myself,
For I, too, put myself
On the back burner to be
A wife and mother.

While my husband studied,
I took every middle-of-the-night feeding,
Moved halfway around the world,
Worked to pay his tuition,
Edited every paper.

I gave him my insights, my theories,
My ideas, my companionship.

Although I am unsure about
The scope of my contribution.
I am proud of my husband
(Though if he runs off with his cousin,
I will, like Mileva, take his Nobel Prize money).
I love being a wife and mother,
And yet I miss myself.

When I learned about
Heavenly Mother—
Our Father's helpmeet,
Divine and universal,
Our eternal prototype,
Unseen and unsung—
I wept with joy.

Although theologians debate
The scope of her contribution,
I have no doubt she shared
Herself with Him—
Her insights, her theories,
Her intelligence, her glory,
Her companionship.

She knows what it's like to be
That woman behind the curtain.

Nancy Heiss

Although the world may ignore me,
A woman behind a curtain,
While they may belittle my ideas
Because I'm only a mother,
Only a wife—

And although I'm scorned
When I say I'd like a peek
At the other side of the curtain,
When I say I need more than
Wifehood and motherhood,
When I say I need, also,
To be me—

I know she sees me
Behind the curtain.
I know she loves me
With or without the curtain.
I know she'll applaud me
When I step out from
Behind the curtain.

Paradoxical Glory

HELP THOU MINE UNBELIEF

Every night I check to see
If my children are still breathing,
If that pipe we fixed is still holding.

I replay conversations in my mind.
Did I say something stupid?
Did I offend anybody?

I can never remember
If I locked the front door,
If I turned off the stove.

I'm not sure if I'm doing enough,
If I am enough. And I don't know
If fairies are real.

But I want to believe.

If you believe, clap your hands!

Clap for the fairies.
Clap for me.
Clap for you.

Please clap.

Nancy Heiss

WITH CHILD

"I just don't think
She should bring her sin
to church," he scoffed.

Her . . . sin?

Oh. Her baby.

A baby is many things,
But not a sin, never a sin.

A baby is a cute, chubby
Consequence. Fine.

A baby is a life-changing
Surprise. Sometimes.

A baby is a heaven-sent
Blessing. Definitely.

A baby is a child of
God. Never a sin.

"I just don't think . . ."

I agree.

IS IT I?

I turned up my nose
At the hazy view
Across the valley from me.

Things seemed fine
In my valley. Happy.

It was only after
I reached the summit
That I noticed the smog.

Choking the life
Out of my valley.
Sad.

Nancy Heiss

TROPHY WIFE

Shrouded in the secrecy
Of a foreign tongue,
And an endless supply of saris,
My friend's grandmother
Seemed to me an enigma.

I understood very little of what she said
But my friend passed all sorts of
Second-hand wisdom to me
From her grandmother.

"I am never breastfeeding my babies!"
My friend told me one day.

"Why not?" I needed to know.

"Because I was showering with Dadiji
And I noticed her boobs were sagging
And when I asked why she said it was
From feeding her children," she said,
Wrinkling her nose with disgust.

"Well, I'm still breastfeeding my babies!"
I told her, unafraid.

"You'll have saggy boobs," she warned.

Half a lifetime,
Five pregnancies and
A decade of breastfeeding later,
Her prophecy came true:

I have saggy breasts,
Stretch marks,
Spider veins . . .

Dadiji never spoke to me in English,
But I understood her in love.
She was a doting grandmother,
So proud of her children and
Her children's children.

I'm sure Dadiji's words were
Not a warning
But a content reflection.

You see my sagging breasts,
Tired skin, greying hair?

It's from growing my babies.
It's from feeding my babies.
It's from loving my babies.

Nancy Heiss

THE LAST WEANING

Is this how Jack's cow felt?

Old and tired
Dried up
Useless
And so sad.

Am I good for nothing now?

Trade me in
For magic
Beans!

Do those even exist?

Perhaps.

Buried deep
Inside of me—
Once upon a time—
There was a dream
A wish, a plan.

I hope it sprouts.
Now that the cow's untethered,
Now that the milk's gone.

BEAUTY FOR ASHES

I admit I was nervous
To meet what I thought
Was his replacement,
As if his former self had dissolved,
And this new visage was a stranger,
Completely unknown by me.

Instead they softly settled
Onto the chair beside mine.

"So, what's new with you?"

"Not much," I answered.
"Except I have five kids now.
What's new with you?"

"Same," she laughed.

crickets

"Except without the kids," she tacked on.

"I heard you let the kids help pick out his name,"
She said, nodding to the newest one, in my arms.

"We did," I admitted.

"I like his name," she said.

"Me, too," I said.
"I kind of wanted Nicholas.
But no one else liked it.

Nancy Heiss

I thought I'd call him Nixie,
After Grandpa. Arnold
Isn't my favourite name,
But he went by Nix as a boy.
Did you know that?"

"I didn't," she said, her eyes sparkling,
Her soul piqued by our shared family history.

And in that moment I realized
(Why did I need to realize?) that
This person isn't a stranger,
Nor is she a replacement.
We grew up together.
We shared a childhood,
Relatives, memories.

I may never understand completely
But it's not my job to understand.

I am here to love,
To give beauty for ashes,
The oil of joy for mourning,
To help her feel God's love
Because she is God's child.

GIVE THEM A NAME

She skipped down the street
Pointing to plants,
And naming them.

Baby sage!
Lamb's-ear!
Pink lady!

She knows names are power.

Nancy Heiss

TO SAMPSON

I never knew my sixth-great grandfather,
But he knew you.

He ripped you from your past,
Away from a mother who loved you.
He hobbled your future,
Maimed every chance,
Silenced every opportunity.
He used you, abused you.
Finally, he put you in his will,
Alongside his sorrel mare:

"My negro man Sampson," he called you.

He gave you away because
He thought he owned you.
Because society allowed it.

I never knew my fifth-great grandfather
And I certainly never knew you,
But, Sampson, I think about you
Every day. And every day
I'm sorry.

AND A BLESSING

She skipped down the street
Chasing fireflies,
And naming them.

Butter!
Jack'n'Jill!
Mr. Flashy Pants!

She knows names are a blessing.

REDACTED

My great-great-great-grandfather,
Edson Barney, is of such great-great renown—
Zion's Camp! First Quorum of the Seventy!
Missions! Missions! Missions!—
His FamilySearch record
Is locked-down:

"This person's record is read-only.
No additions or changes can be made."

Nancy Heiss

In his autobiography
Edson portrays his life
As perfectly monogamous.

He speaks of Lillis Ballou, his first wife,
Who would bear him seven children.

He ignores his second wife,
My great-great-great-grandmother,
Louisa Walker, who bore him nine.

No mention of a second wife
Or those many other children.

No Louisa Walker, and thus
No Lillis Louisa,
No Celia May,
No Zetta Pearl,
No Myrna June,
No me.

Risk-averse, afraid of shame,
This great-great man
Blotted an entire family line
Out of his narrative,
But we live to tell
Our own great stories.

VICTIM OF FERTILITY

My grandma got married
And had child
After child
After child
After child
After child
After child
After child

They came so rapidly
She began to wonder how
They came to be at all.

Must have slept
Through it,
She said.

She was so tired
From all those
Children.

Nancy Heiss

MY BOX OF CHOCOLATES

My first baby was born with a headful of
Beautiful, dark hair. She slept a little.
She cried a lot. She was always in a hurry
To roll, to crawl, to walk, to talk.

My second baby was blonde as could be.
She was quite the sight to behold in
Her birthplace; in Egypt. She was so content.
She sucked her thumb until kindergarten.

My third baby surprised us by coming early.
He had the world's most fluffy hair—
Brown until his first haircut, then blonde.
Over energetic; he continues to surprise us.

My fourth baby came out bald and scowling;
Colicky, categorically unimpressed, sleepless.
Her first three years were spent alternately
Screaming and singing about everything.

My fifth baby was a wonder from the start.
He seems to genuinely enjoy sleeping, which
I can hardly wrap my head around, given my
Previous experience. We're still getting to know him.

"You never can tell," a doctor once told me.
"What you'll get when you shake the tree of life."

Nancy Heiss

REMEMBRANCE

At my 20-week ultrasound
I rejoiced when I saw
Ten fingers, ten toes,
Her kidneys, her heart.

Then they showed me her head
And all I could think was:

"That is a human skull"; and,
"It has to come out of me."

MOMMY BRAINSTORMING

Since giving birth
My brain is capable only of
Twitter-like thoughts:
280 characters or fewer.

MYTHOS

When a child is born
A mother is ~~born, too~~
Primally summoned.

Split at perineum or navel,
She breathes new life
Into the world.

Each surge of pressure,
Reveals her fierceness.

Each urge to push
Reveals her power.

She is transformed.

A warrior.
A goddess.
A mother.

Nancy Heiss

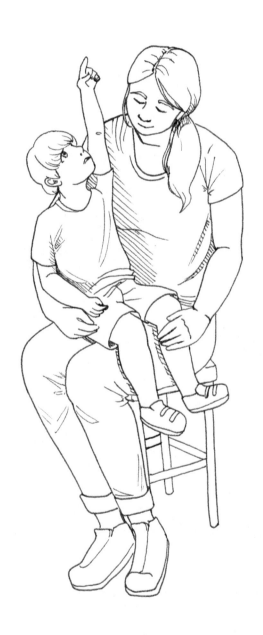

RUNNER UP II

He told me:
You're the second-best mom in the universe.
Because who's the first? Come on—guess!

Heavenly Mother?

Yes. Heavenly Mother.

THE BIRTH STORY

I asked him to tell me
What he remembered
Of his sister being born.

"Can I just draw a picture
Of Heavenly Father
Handing her to you?"
He asked.

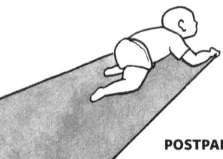

POSTPARTUM DEPRESSION

Can your baby hold his or her head up well? Yes.
Does your baby play on his or her stomach? Yes.
Do you make an effort to talk to your baby
 whenever possible? Yes.
Are your other children adjusting okay with
 the new baby? Yes.

Are you enjoying your baby?

Yes or No?

. . .
. . .
. . .

Yes or No?

. . .
. . .
. . .

Yes . . . ?

Or no . . . ?

Paradoxical Glory

PEACE BY PIECE

When the phone rang; he answered
The remote control instead.
He couldn't remember my name,
Or whether it was time for
Breakfast, or lunch, or dinner.

But he remembered God.

"Thou wilt keep him in perfect peace,"
His scraggly letters testified,
"Whose mind is stayed on thee,
Because he trusteth in thee."

And he trusted God.

It was fitting he found comfort there,
In perfect, persistent peace—
Shalom wa-shalom!
Peace and peace!—
Too constant to forget.

Thus he relied on God.

"Spiritual stability," he wrote,
"Works against mental instability."
Faith didn't fix his memory
But it spoke peace to his soul.

Nancy Heiss

Is it the same for me, God?
The anxiety that plagues me
Feels real but is unfounded.
Is it possible I'm surrounded
By peace that I can't feel?

Don't give up on me, God.

I'm right here, behind this wall.
There's no door, no window,
But perhaps together we
Can chip away at things

Peace by piece, God,
Shalom wa-shalom.

JUST RIGHT

Goldilocks saw Baby Bear's
Everything as "just right."

His oatmeal, his chair, his bed.

Baby Bear felt
Everything was wrong.

Empty, broken, crowded.

Motherhood can leave you
Feeling hopelessly alone
And relentlessly over-touched.

Motherhood can feel at once
Like too much and
Not enough.

But you are enough
For motherhood.

You are just right.

BE YE THEREFORE PERFECT

My baby was born imperfect.
Ten beautiful fingers,
Ten beautiful toes,
But imperfect—
He struggles to breathe.

I love every bit of him.
His ten tiny fingers,
His ten tiny toes,
The raspy way
He gasps for air.

Still, I pray for my baby
To learn to breathe,
To breathe easy.

He taught me that
God loves me, wholly,
Not in spite of my
Imperfections,
But with them.

Every bit of me is loveable.

But still God wants me
To learn, to grow,
To become
Perfect.

Nancy Heiss

COME UNTO ME

All ye who labour
And are heavy laden:

Give me your empty bowls,
Your broken chairs, the
Sleepless nights you spent
Being kicked by all those
Little feet tucked into
Your overcrowded bed.
Give me your best,
Imperfect offerings.

I will give you rest.

LITTLE FISH

She dove into the water
With full confidence
And swam to me
Without any
Instruction.

She grinned underwater,
Her eyes curious yet calm,
Elated to be submerged.

I lifted her up, I praised her:
Told her she was brave,
That she did a good job.

I told her to breathe.

I didn't say that she'd been
Drowning the entire time.

I only told her to breathe
Now that she was safe in my arms.

Please, God, don't let me drown.

Nancy Heiss

IN MY MOTHER'S ARMS

"Carry me, please!"
My baby said.
And so I scooped him up.

Then, "Carry me, please!"
He said again, though I
Held him in my arms.

Carry me, please!

I am. I am.

Carry me, please!

I am.

Carry me, please!

I am, my child.
I am. I am. I am.

I AM

"Carry me, please,"
I cried in prayer.

The wind whispered,
I Am.

"Carry me, please,"
I begged again.

And the sun smiled down
I Am.

"Carry me, please."

The sky Her eyes,
The rain Her tears,
The earth Her gentle arms.

Carry me, please!
Oh, carry me!

I Am. I Am. I Am.

Nancy Heiss

A CHILD'S PRAYER

Don't go!
Stay here—
Be my mommy.

THE LAST BABY

His reluctance to walk
Makes me think
He knows I need him
To need me
A little bit longer.

Nancy Heiss

THE DOOR

We have passed the point
Of complete meltdowns
When I disappear behind
The bathroom door.

Instead he shoves offerings
Beneath the door—
Matchbox cars,
Primitive drawings,
And bouncy balls—
Enticing me to play.

His little fingers appear:
Wiggling
Reaching
Yearning.

"Mama! Mama!"

He can't see me.
But he knows I am there.

He trusts I'll come out soon.

Nancy Heiss

SOS

Before he uttered a single word,
My baby learned to sign the word milk.

His pudgy fingers frantically pulsed
Open and closed, open and closed.

— —   • •   • — • •   — • —

"The baby's hands are flashing again,"
His big sister would announce,
As if he were attempting to
Communicate with us
In Morse code.

— —   • •   • — • •   — • —

"I think you need to feed him."

Of course I did. He was always hungry.
But not always for milk.

— —   • •   • — • •   — • —

He was hungry for
The sound of my voice,
The touch of my skin,
The thrum of my heart.

— —   • •   • — • •   — • —

All of it was milk for him.

• • •   — — —   • • •

Paradoxical Glory

Sometimes words escape me when I pray
And all I can do is pour out the contents of my heart:

My love, my hope, my joy, my gratitude,
My pain, my sorrow, my anger, my fears.

• • •   – – –   • • •

"Please," I say, "take this."
And my heart pounds out a
Message I can't find
The words for.

• • •   – – –   • • •

I need you.

• • •   – – –   • • •

Nancy Heiss

MILK MUSIC

As he nursed, the baby hummed.

"Why are you humming, baby?"
His sister asked. He didn't respond,
Because he was nursing, but
He hummed a little louder.

"Why are you humming?
Why is he humming, Mom?"
She turned her question to me.

Because he is happy, I suppose,
I told her.

"Well, that sounds really great, baby.
You should hum more often.
You should make music."

It's the song of his heart.

LACTATIONAL AMENORRHEA

When I grow weary of
Middle-of-the-night feedings,
I remember what I'm delaying.

Can I get an amen?

Nancy Heiss

MIDNIGHT FEEDINGS AND FAMILY PLANNING

Imagine doing this all over again.
But, oh, imagine *not* doing it again.

BOMBS AWAY

The oak tree is launching
Acorns—missiles of life—
That take time—
Days
Weeks
Years
Centuries—
To fully explode.

I ONCE WAS BLIND

I didn't know how little I saw
Until at church my mom asked me
To tell her the hymn number.

She thought I was being impudent
When I told her I didn't know.

Just look at the numbers
And tell me, she said.

Nancy Heiss

What numbers? Where?

Up front.

Where?

There.

Where? Mom, there
Are no numbers there.

She promptly made an
Appointment with the
Optometrist and
When I put on my glasses
I was amazed at what
I could see.

Leaves on the trees
Cracks on the sidewalk
Street signs, people's faces,
The hymn board
At the front of
The chapel.

And I've never stopped wondering
How I lived so long without seeing.

Paradoxical Glory

BRCA

At eleven years old
I was thrilled
To see death sprout
On my chest

RUSSIAN SUPERSTITIONS

Before I climbed into their Lada,
My host parents carefully
Arranged stacks of blankets
On the backseat for me to sit on—
Princess-and-the-pea style.
To keep my ovaries
From freezing, they said.

It must have worked.

ACCIDENTAL CAT LADY

I tore open the wrapping paper
To reveal a ceramic cat. Again.

"Oh, wow," I faltered,
Trying to feign surprise.
"A . . . cat."

Every year it was the same—
On my birthday I got a ceramic cat.

"What's wrong?" Mom asked.
"Don't you like it?"

"Oh, sure," I replied. "It's just . . ."

"What?"

"Why does everyone keep giving me cats?"

"Because you collect them."

I didn't. Not really.
I had them, of course.
I had a lot of them.

But only because they kept coming.

Nancy Heiss

COLLECTIONS

My brother collected fascinating things:
Sports cards, stamps, coins.

I tried following in his footsteps but
He didn't welcome the competition.

Eventually my mom told me
To find my own passion.

I tried collecting bugs and rocks.
No one wanted those things in the house.

My ceramic cat collection was thrill-less.
Stuffed animals? Too big. Too boring.

So I began collecting pencils.

I amassed hundreds of bedazzled pencils.

Pencils emblazoned with school emblems.
Pencils with rainbow-coloured lead.
Pencils with crazy toppers.

It was lame, but don't laugh:
My mom had a napkin collection.

SOUVENIR

When I was nine my family moved
Across the Rocky Mountains.

To fuel excitement, my teacher
Brought province pencils to school.

He gave me all the Alberta ones
When what I really wanted was
One that said British Columbia
Because that was my home.

I wanted proof that I had come
From somewhere else.

I've now moved so many times
I've stopped trying to explain
Where I'm from because I can't.

I wish I had proof that I had come
From somewhere else.
But everything I have is
Stamped with Earth.

I have no pencils from heaven.

Nancy Heiss

RAIN SHADOW

Prevailing winds and
Constant storms seem
Hard and cruel
Until you learn that
Little blooms on
The leeward slope.

I WATCHED MY MOTHER GROW UP

I remember cheering for my mother
When she accepted her diploma,
Having finally earned her degree.
I was nine years old; my sister—a baby.

My mother, bachelor of the arts.

Later I watched her devour books,
Collect quotes on cue cards,
And, eventually, type her thesis
On MS-DOS, old-school style.

My mother, master of the arts.

A few years later she was at it again.
Read, study, write. Wash, rinse, repeat.
Another day, another degree,
A better chance to provide for her family.

My mother, master of science.

Her thirst for knowledge unabated,
My mother tackled a PhD.
She allowed me, with my dastardly red pen,
To review her dissertation; it was good.

My mother, doctor of philosophy.

THERE SHALL BE A RECORD KEPT AMONG YOU

Zoë's book, she carefully scrawled,
Page after page after page.

Not being sure how to write
Being a record of my people

Not being sure how to write
I give an account of my proceedings

Not being sure how to write
It must needs be that I write a little

Not being sure how to write.

Nevertheless, having been taught
Somewhat in the language of her mother
She wrote and she wrote and she wrote—
Hidden away under her covers,
By the illicit glow of flashlight:

Zoë's book.
Zoë's book.
Zoë's book.

Nancy Heiss

FINDING MY VOICE

At age two I fell
And broke my arm,
Then silently cradled
My injured limb.

I attended classes
At BYU with my mom,
And sat under her desk
Quietly munching Fruit Loops.

At age four I refused
To say a word to my
Babysitter. Ever.

She asked my mom if I
Even knew how to talk.

I stood beside my mother
And thought about how
Ridiculous that question was.

Of course I knew how to speak;
I just didn't—or couldn't—
Speak to her.

I wonder if I am why
She became a
Speech pathologist.

At age six my older sister
Disappeared and
My once steady world
Descended into chaos.

Missing child posters.
Police cars at my house.
Worry and tears and anger.

I was sent to the school psychologist.
She had lovely stickers—sparkly ones
And puffy ones, scratch-and-sniff ones—
But I didn't—or couldn't—tell her much.

My teacher told me
To write instead.

So page after page,
With a pencil in my hand—
My letters still backwards,
Misshapen and shaky—
I sounded out my world.

For the very first time.

Nancy Heiss

LOVE LETTERS

Is it any wonder
That I fell in love
With my husband
Through letters?

Writing is where
I am my truest self.

And he had the
Most beautiful
Words in return.

Nancy Heiss

A FIRST DATE

He pulled out his scriptures,
With the colour-coded index
And proudly flipped through it.

"Do you have a scripture-marking system?" he asked.

I do.

I mark whatever I want
However I want to
In that very moment.

"So not a system," he observed.

I guess not.

He has been trying to be
The order to my chaos
Ever since.

THE DREAM CATCHER

I grew up believing dreams
Were beautiful but useless.
Nice to have, but upon waking
They'd abandon you to reality.

I must be careful what I say
Around my husband, then,
For he is a dream catcher.

As soon as I give my dream a voice,
He snatches it and holds it fast,
Transforms it into a blueprint,
This engineer of dreams.

"Why not?" he'll ask. "You should!"
He'll say, "Let's make a plan."
"Do it! It's not too late!"

There is an art to following
Your dreams, you know,
A formula of sorts.
You can learn it, but it's hard.

It helps to have a good teacher
And a different sort of dream catcher—
The kind that opens their arms wide
To catch you when you fall awake.

The kind that helps you dream again,
The kind that knows dreams aren't useless.

Nancy Heiss

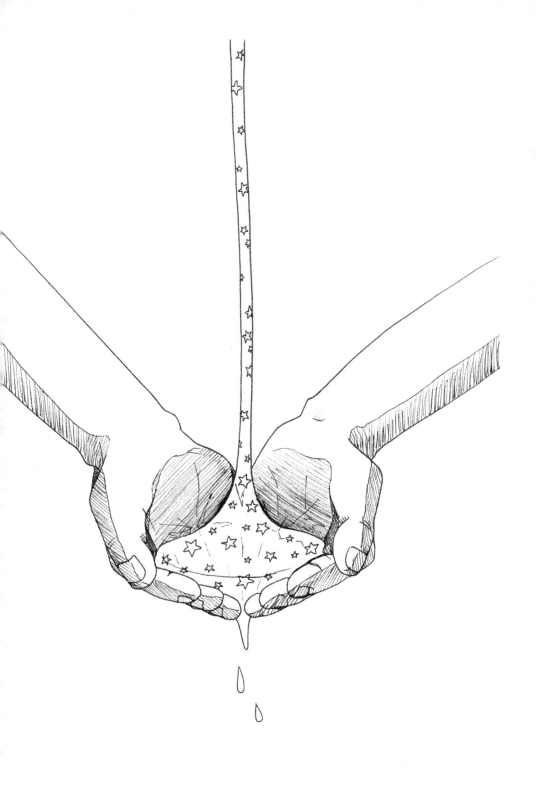

OLD WIVES TALES

The mother said, "Shhhh!
Loud noises will make the cake fall."
And her children played quietly
While the cake was in the oven.

The daughter said, "Shhhh!
Play quietly or the cake will fall."
And her children played quietly
While the cake was in the oven.

So I said, "Shhhh! Be quiet
Or you will ruin my cake!"
And my husband laughed.
"What do you mean?"

I explained that loud noises,
Naturally, will make a cake fall.

"That is not a thing," he said.

So I looked it up;
It's not a thing.

I told my mom.

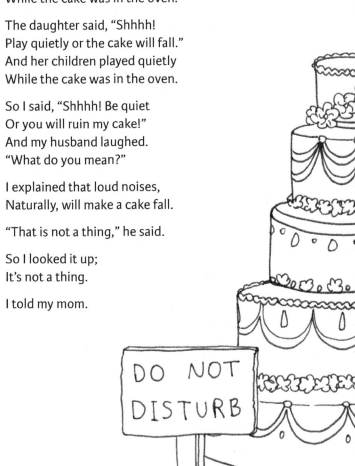

And we wondered together
If her mother had blindly
Passed on knowledge
From her foremothers,
Or if she'd known the truth.

Because I know the truth
And yet I still teach my children
That anything but silence
Will ruin a cake.

My grandmother was a smart woman.

NOT GOOD ENOUGH

"Sweep the floor," my grandma said.
And so I swept the floor.

"Now sweep again," she parroted.
And so I swept it more.

And though she's long since left behind
This toilsome earthly heap,
My soul is not bereft; I find
She's with me when I sweep.

My house is now most feebly swept
By child-driven brooms,
Which leave behind crumbs (I suspect)
And dust flecks in each room.

I gracefully ignore the grime
But hear Gram's spirit blurt:

"You can sweep the floor two times
And still you'll pick up dirt!"

Nancy Heiss

MOP, MOP, MOP

Shoulder to shoulder,
On hands and knees,
We mopped the floor.

There are still crumbs, Momma . . .

Which is precisely why my Grandma
Always said to sweep twice.

You didn't listen, Momma.
Why didn't you listen?

Because long ago I gave up the dream
Of ever having a perfectly clean floor.

And because knowing something
And doing something are
Very different things.

CHORE CHARTS

And it came to pass that I
did cause my people to be industrious,
and to labor with their hands.

And they did murmur against me, saying,
"Aw, Mom. Come on!"

Now I do not write all the words
which they murmured against me.
But it sufficeth me to say that
They did seek to take away my sanity.

ROLE REVERSAL

Miriam informed me that
Coronavirus has affected
More men than women.

"I think," she said, "it's because
Men do the grocery shopping
While the women stay at home."

Oh, sweetie.

Nancy Heiss

GENDER ROLES

He works full-time
And grocery shops.
Gets the oil changed,
Mows the lawn and
Pays the bills.
Does the laundry,
Cooks the best meals,
Vacuums, bakes,
And takes the kids
To the orthodontist.

She stays home with the kids
And cleans the toilets.
Changes furnace filters,
Mows the lawn and
Cleans out the gutters.
Does the laundry,
Decorates birthday cakes,
Writes and sweeps,
And takes the kids
To the doctor.

They do the things
That need to be done.

RENTED SPACES

If this place were really mine
I'd paint the walls,
Reorganize—
Find a place for everything.

But my time here is finite
And I have things to do.

BAPTIST TESTIMONY

Maribelle wore a great big hat
To church each Sunday.

Florid pink,
Bold purple,
Or turquoise.
Bedazzled
With sequins
And feathers
And ribbons
And lace.

When she got up to bear her testimony
She almost danced to the pulpit, singing
About how she's glad Jesus lifted her
Or how she's gonna live so God can use her
Or how she planned to let her little light shine, shine, shine.

I don't remember a word she said
But I remember her music
I remember her light.

MOVING ON

I spent the afternoon erasing . . .
Errant pencil marks
Something sticky
Tiny, grimy fingerprints
Crusted-on boogers
Too many scuff marks
. . . off my empty walls.

They said that I would miss this,
The wise ones who came before.
They said that I would miss this:
The messes
The handprints
The toys on the floor.

I spent the afternoon retracing . . .
Leftover hugs and giggles
Evidence of growing inches
Bickering and name-calling
Dripping sniffles in timeout
Echoes of love, of beauty
. . . off my empty walls.

Nancy Heiss

I didn't think I'd miss this
While the kids are still so small.
I tell them it's okay to miss this:
The house
Their bedroom
It's okay to miss it all.

I spent the afternoon replacing . . .
Memories and daydreams
A newborn's mewling
Birthday candle shadows
One-of-a-kind artwork
Proof of my family, of joy
. . . with nothing on my empty walls.

SETTLING IN

The family that lived here before
Had eight children, I'm told.

"Eight! And they ran a tight ship,"
I'm told. Unsaid words hang in the air.
"And clearly you do not," they taunt.

Me, with my mismatched furniture.
Me, with my mountains of unfolded laundry.
Me, with Lego strewn about my basement.
Me, with toothpaste gobs in my sink.
Me, with dinner droppings under my table.
Me, with splotches of spit up on everything I own.
Me, with the disheveled-looking children:
Sun kissed hair, head-to-toe in hand-me-downs,
Pants on backwards or inside out (or not at all),
Leftover lunch lurking around their smiles (or frowns).

The carefree but volatile preteen,
The tattle-telling eight-year-old,
The bouncing-off-the-walls kindergartener,
The screaming toddler, the fussing baby.

Five. Just five of them.
And look at this place!
It's a zoo, I'll give you that.

They had eight. And they ran a tight ship.

Sure they did. Super tight.
Tight, like unto-a-dish tight.

But the walls of this home hold secrets
And they whisper them to me.

The hole in the wall where someone—
Not any of us—opened a door too forcefully.
The crusty neon green stuff—of unknown origin—
On the carpet upstairs that won't come off.
The loose baluster on the staircase that will.
The dog scratches on the front door
(We've never had a dog).

The plethora of straight pins I've found
Lodged within the ancient fibres of
The shag carpet in the basement,
Where a previous crafter spilled a collection of
Miniscule beads (which make a racket
Every time I vacuum).

Scribbles on the inside of a closet door.
Water stains under the kitchen sink.
The broken screen in a bedroom window.
The big letter M etched into a panel
Of the disheveled venetian blinds.

You may have seen perfection in this
Ship-shape, tight-as-a-dish family
with eight children—eight!—
But their home tells a different story,
A messier story, a Noah's Ark story.

A story like mine.

MY FRAIL EXISTENCE

"Are you looking forward
to going back home?" she asked.

"Home's relative," I answered.

Home is wherever you make it,
So I was going home, I suppose.
But this was a new adventure,
A brand-new chapter of my life.
There was no back about it.

"Some people thrive living abroad,"
She sniffed. "And some people don't.
You belong in the latter category
So I'm glad you're going home."

She was right that I didn't belong there
But she was wrong that I belonged
To the next leg in my journey.

Having wandered from a more exalted sphere
I have never felt that I belong to this journey.
Rather, this journey belongs to me.

I'm not sure I've thrived living abroad
—here—
But I've done my best.

And I think I will be glad to go home.

Nancy Heiss

MY THOUGHTS ≠ YOUR THOUGHTS

Six words ran through
My mind. Not my words,
Not my thoughts:

This is how we lose her.

Six words foretold
An unavoidable tragedy.

This is how we lose her.

Nothing was wrong . . . yet.
Not terribly. All was well.

This is how we lose her.

This is how we lose her?
Pneumonia?

This is how we lose her . . .
Years down the road,
I reasoned.

I grossly miscalculated
Their urgency.

This. Is. How. We. Lose. Her.

Six words ran through
My mind. Not my words,
Not my thoughts.

Not foreshadowing.
A notification.

This. Is. How. We. Lose. Her.

Plain potent words
I couldn't make sense of—
O feeble mind!—
Until the meaning was
Revealed; the words came true.

This is how we lost her.

Nancy Heiss

I DON'T WANT THIS SADNESS

I have watched Death creep
Inch . . . by inch . . . by inch . . .
Until, finally,
It makes its move,
Bringing grief,
But also relief.

I have seen Death rob
Cradles, wombs, wedding beds.
Striking randomly,
It leaves in its wake
Anguish, sorrow,
Pain-filled tomorrows.

I have known Death from afar,
As a fact of life, as clinical.
It has taken—family,
Friends, strangers—
Slowly and sudden,
This angel unbidden.

I hear Death knocking
At my door—not for me—
For one I love.

I don't want this sadness.

It's time to learn, Death says.

Come in.

Paradoxical Glory

THEY CAME RUNNING

At midnight they came running,
A pack of feral mourners
Bursting into the ICU:

The babies in their jammies,
Sleep clinging to their eyes,
Arms clinging to their grandpa.

The six-year-old in Sunday slacks
And a brand new t-shirt—stickers on front
Proclaiming 6T 6T 6T 6T 6T,
Sales tag dangling out the back.

The nine-year-old in sock feet;
She'd forgotten about shoes entirely.

The eleven-year-old in an oversized t-shirt,
Kleenex stuffed up her nostrils
To stanch her runny nose.

Auntie Em, with her shirt on inside out.

At midnight they flew
Out of their beds
To her bedside
To say goodbye.

Nancy Heiss

Paradoxical Glory

BURNT OFFERINGS

I opened the door
And there she stood,
A foil-wrapped plate
In her outstretched hands.

I knew it would be neither
Delicious nor at all desirable.

She was not a good cook.

But I took the plate and
Offered my thanks.

Her now-empty arms
Wrapped me in a hug
As we stood together
In the doorway.

We wept.

"Oh, how I love her!"
She cried. "Is there
Nothing that can be done?"

Nothing. Her blood has
Turned to poison.

"If she needs blood,
I will donate mine!"

Nancy Heiss

No use. Too late.

We wept.

And wept,

And wept,

Then pulled away.
We wiped our noses.
We blotted our eyes.

"If there's anything I can do . . ."

I'll let you know . . .

The cookies were dry.
Overdone. And perfect—
A vehicle for true service.

I didn't need a cookie;
I needed to be wept with.

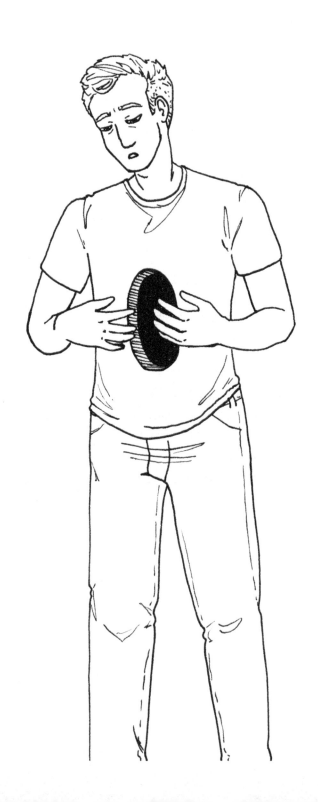

OBJECT PERMANENCE

They bring us food, I think, to remind us we're alive,
And a hug to remind us we are loved.

Coaxing us out of our numb stupor
They fill us with comfort, inside and out.

And we take it eagerly,
Greedily. Like a colicky infant

Who needs his mother's arms around him
and his mother's milk inside him.

His thirst unquenchable
As he discovers temporal object permanence;

Our hole unfathomable
As we navigate celestial object permanence.

COOKIES FOR THE SAD

"Where are the sad people?" the child asked.

"Oh, baby. There are sad people
all over the world," said her mother.

"We should bring them a cookie," said the child.

CRUSHED VELVET

When Maribelle saw us
She rushed at us
With arms and smile wide.

She crushed us into
Her crushed velvet dress,
More purple than purple.

"I'm so sorry 'bout your momma!"
She crooned, tears glistening in her eyes.

It was a heavenly,
Rib-crushing,
Soul-soothing,
Purple velvet hug.

Nancy Heiss

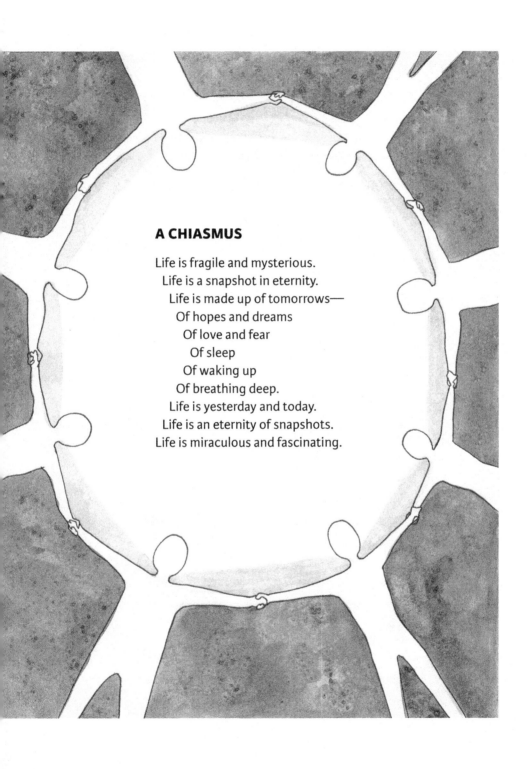

A CHIASMUS

Life is fragile and mysterious.
 Life is a snapshot in eternity.
  Life is made up of tomorrows—
   Of hopes and dreams
    Of love and fear
     Of sleep
     Of waking up
    Of breathing deep.
   Life is yesterday and today.
  Life is an eternity of snapshots.
 Life is miraculous and fascinating.

A BEDTIME PRAYER

Dear Heavenly Father
My grandma was sick
And now she is dead
We are so sad
In the name of Jesus Christ
Amen

PEN PALS

I am writing a letter to Grandma.
Is Grandma writing a letter to me?
I just know she is.
Do you know if they have paper and pencils
In heaven? Or maybe she brought her own.

Nancy Heiss

**MIRIAM'S WORRY
(AND THE ANSWER)**

"I can't remember
The last thing
She said to me."

Whatever it was,
It meant
I love you.

THE INFINITY SCARF

She begged me
To finish the scarf
Her grandmother
Started decades ago.

We found it in a box—
A tangled mass of
Christmas-red yarn.

I worked through each knot,
Counted her stitches,
Decoded the pattern,
And picked up
Where she
Left off.

I did my best to tie up
Her loose ends.

But you can tell
Where her handiwork ends
And my stitches begin.

Her stitches—cozy and carefree,
Mine—tight and well-behaved.

Nancy Heiss

A seamless demarcation
Between what's mine and hers,
Connecting me to her.

When it was long enough
I joined the ends together.

One loop, two artists, one wearer.

"I love it!" my daughter told me.

And she wore it every day for months—
Carefully coordinated
Or flagrantly mismatched
With her outfit,
Depending on the day.

A bit of me, a bit of Grandma
Orbiting her, always.

A WELL-INTENDED LADY

I sorted through her good intentions—
Unfinished quilts
Half-knitted scarves
Forgotten needlework
A set of matching outfits—
Cut, but not sewn—
For three little girls
Long-since grown.

Small in number compared to
The countless intentions
She carried out.

Nancy Heiss

DECONSTRUCTION

We rifled through her life,
Page by page, deciding
What to keep and
What to toss.

One childhood diary,
Marked "secret" and
Willed to her best friend
On the front pastedown?

Keep.

One folder of photocopies
From a Relief Society
Recipe Exchange?

Toss.

Letters from her first—
And fleeting—engagement?

Keep.

Minutes from 1980s HOA
Meetings, for which she was
The treasurer?

Toss.

Journals from college and her mission,
Her yearnings to find a husband, then,
Upon finally finding one, chronicling
Her early years as wife and mother?

Keep.

An album entirely devoted to YW Camp
That does not feature a single photo of her?

Toss.

Keep.

Keep.

Toss.

Sneaking glimpses of who she once was,
Pawing through her private records,
Devouring her intimate thoughts,
Piecing together a narrative.

Finding answers to questions
We never asked,
That we can't ask now.

Finding questions
We didn't know
We should have asked
When we could have.

Deciding how to present her

Nancy Heiss

To future generations.

Which breadcrumbs do we keep?

Which clues do we toss?

The pattern for the picnic table
On the patio, which she made?

Toss.

One set of scriptures, leather
Worn soft from years of use,
A colour-coded scripture-marking system
On the end pages?

Keep.

FOOD STORAGE

For months after she died
We continued to eat
The peaches—
Canned, jammed,
And dehydrated—
Which she helped put up
The month before she died.

Nancy Heiss

FOUR-GENERATION HONEY

George harvested honey
Decades ago and drizzled it—
Drip by glistening golden drip—
Into old jars from pickles,
Mayonnaise,
Spaghetti sauce,
Which he stored in his garage.

Passed down from
Generation to generation
The honey grew dark and thick
And darker and thicker still
Until we found it
In the pantry,
Pried off the lid,
Warmed it so that
It oozed once again,
And spread it on toast.

We told the kids:
This honey is older
Than all of us,

This honey your great-grandfather
Gave to your grandmother,
Who gave it to your father,
Who gave it to you.

PHANTOM PAINS

Sometimes, after I've removed my glasses,
I reach up to adjust them

To find they're not there.

Sometimes, after a haircut,
I squirt out way too much shampoo

For hair that's not there.

Sometimes, after you're gone,
I pull a plate out of the cupboard for you

But you're not here.

I'm not forgetful;
I remember too well.

Nancy Heiss

I SEE DEAD PEOPLE

"Your memories from this week last year . . ."
The email subject warned me.

I clicked on it, and there she was,
Smiling, holding my baby.

She was his Grandma for a year.
Now she visits only in our memories.

Now when he sees her picture
He says, "Who's that?"

THE FIRST HOLIDAY WITHOUT YOU

It was an odd Thanksgiving.
Bereft of gloom.
Bereft of joy.
Bereft
Of everything
But emptiness.

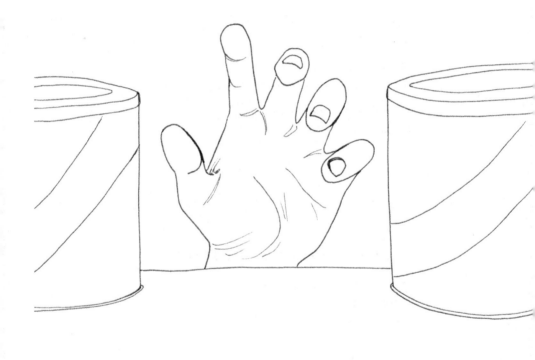

MISSING MOTHER

The first Christmas
After she died
He bought hot chocolate.

Peppermint.
Cookies'n'cream.
Orange.
Cinnamon.

Every flavour imaginable.

He didn't even drink it,
Not much, anyway.
He just bought it.

Salted caramel.
Chocolate raspberry.
Hazlenut.
Extra dark.

Every flavour imaginable.

Stacked in the cupboard,
Just taking up space
That had been left empty.

FINDING MOTHER

The second Christmas
After she died
He built things.

Gingerbread houses,
Tree houses.

He'd never touched
An icing bag
Or a table saw
His whole life.

But she had,
So he did.

He found his mother
In powdered sugar
And sawdust.

Nancy Heiss

CHRISTMAS YET TO COME

"I don't put a tree up these days,"
Grandpa said.

"Yeah, I just do the train.
She always did the tree.
I always did the train.
So now there's no tree."

And I wonder if, one day,
When my grandkids
Bring their kids
To visit me

Will there only be a train?
Will there only be a tree?

Nancy Heiss

WE, THE RISING GENERATION

One by one her siblings passed
Until she was the only one left
In her generation—
My grandmother.

When she died my mom cried,
"We're orphans."

My aunt whispered,
"We're next."

Back then "next" seemed
So far away and
I couldn't understand
How grown-ups could be
Orphans.

Not too many years later,
Orphanhood lurks
Around the corner.

I'm not ready
To be next.

But we're up.

WITHER AND BLOOM

Five times my belly
Has swelled—with life, creation—
Then deflated with birth.

Five times my skin has stretched,
Been etched with a gossamer
Script. Your signature.

Five times my breasts grew
Large, filled to bursting with milk,
Then sagged—weaned and empty.

Five times my mind felt
Lost. Hazy from sleepless nights.
Depressed. Atrophied.

I am more than just
A withered, empty vessel,
More than a milk cow.

I am more than a
Stretch-marked, pock-marked
Shipment container.

There's still creation in me.
Watch closely, you'll see—
I'll blossom again.

For I am a mother
Of more than just children.
I am mother of all my creations.

Nancy Heiss

NOTES

LOOKING DOWN Inspired in part by Carl B. Cook's retelling of a pep talk President Monson gave him in his October 2011 General Conference address, "It is Better to Look Up."

SOMETHING EXTRAORDINARY Emma Smith, Sarah Cleveland, Eliza Snow in *Relief Society Minute Book*, Nauvoo, Illinois, Mar. 17, 1842, Church History Library, Salt Lake City, 12.

HOW GREAT SHALL BE YOUR JOY D&C 18:15–16. "And if it so be that you should labor all your days in crying repentance unto this people, and bring, save it be one soul until me, how great shall by your joy with him in the kingdom of my Father! And now, if your joy will be great with one soul that you have brought unto me into the kingdom of my Father, how great will be your joy if you should bring many souls unto me!"

PREFERENCES With thanks to Rachel Hunt Steenblik, who taught me that lessons are found everywhere.

HELP THOU MINE UNBELIEF Inspired by Mark 9:24. *Peter Pan* by J.M. Barrie, chapter 13. And Jeb Bush's plea during the 2016 Republican Presidential Primary Campaign.

BEAUTY FOR ASHES For my beautiful cousin, Ash.

GIVE THEM A NAME Inspired by Miriam.

TO SAMPSON Inspired by the will of Samuel C. "Big" Weathers, Sr. (1745–29 November 1819) of Lincoln County, Georgia.

I wouldn't say that I feel guilt over the actions of this ancestor. However, I do see how generations of my family have benefited because of how they obtained and worked their land and acquired wealth while trampling the human rights of others. So I think I am responsible for helping ensure the civil liberties of people who have been crying out for mercy and justice for generations.

AND A BLESSING   Inspired by Zoë.

REDACTED   In loving memory of the women in my family who tell the important stories.

VICTIM OF FERTILITY   Inspired by my grandmother, Evon.

THE BIRTH STORY   Inspired by Benjamin.

MYTHOS   Inspired by Rachel, who transformed me.

RUNNER UP II   Inspired by Benjamin.

POSTPARTUM DEPRESSION   Inspired by a well-child visit and how absolutely earth-shatteringly difficult it is to bring life into the world.

PEACE BY PIECE   Isaiah 26:3. "Thou wilt keep him in perfect peace, whose mind is stayed on thee: because he trusteth in thee." In the original Hebrew, the word peace is repeated for emphasis, translated into English as "perfect peace." Shalom wa-shalom. Thank you to Suzanne Tuck for sharing her grandfather's beautiful letters. He helped inspire this poem, along with my grandfather, Wayne, who suffered from Parkinson's disease and dementia.

JUST RIGHT   Thank you, Amy Egbert, for helping me see that this poem should be.

BE YE THEREFORE PERFECT   Matthew 5:48. "Be ye therefore perfect, even as your Father which is in heaven is perfect." Inspired by Alexander and Benjamin.

COME UNTO ME   Inspired by Matthew 11:28, "The New Colossus" by Emma Lazarus, Baby Bear, and tired mothers everywhere.

LITTLE FISH   Inspired by Zoë, who is categorically unafraid of drowning.

IN MY MOTHER'S ARMS and **A CHILD'S PRAYER**   Inspired by Alexander, who is ceaselessly clingy.

SOS   All of my children have loved milk and signed for milk before they could speak. But it was Zoë who declared "the baby's hands are flashing."

MILK MUSIC   Inspired by Alexander and Zoë.

LACTATIONAL AMENORRHEA   An ode to the period of postnatal infertility occurring when breastfeeding delays the return of a woman's menstrual cycle. Worth it.

MIDNIGHT FEEDINGS AND FAMILY PLANNING   Just before this book was published, I ended up having another baby and found myself wishing she could have found her way into this book. My husband pointed out that she was in the book. Here, in my inability to imagine not doing this again. Welcome to the world, Phoebe.

BRCA Especially for my cousin Bev and her sweet girls. But also for the many other women (and men) in my family affected by the BRCA2 mutation (and/or who have battled breast cancer with no known genetic mutation), specifically my grandmothers on both sides, Aunt Edna, Aunt Lillis, Aunt Celia, Aunt Tami, Auntie Arlene, etc. And for my friends walking this same long road. It's an ever-growing hitlist.

RUSSIAN SUPERSTITIONS For Sasha, Oxcana and Alyosha for taking such good care of me. And for Tatiana and Sergei, who had the best cherry kompot and who would never let me sit at the corner of a table. They are the reason I am not an old maid.

I WATCHED MY MOTHER GROW UP For my beautiful, hard-working, faithful mother.

THERE SHALL BE A RECORD KEPT AMONG YOU Inspired by D&C 21:1, 1 Nephi 1:17, 1 Nephi 19:1, Jarom 1:2, and Zoë.

A FIRST DATE My husband and I went on our first date mere hours after he was released from his mission. It was very awkward and he really pulled out his scriptures to show me his scripture-marking system.

THE DREAM CATCHER For Andrew, who is always encouraging me to do things.

OLD WIVES TALES Inspired by my grandmother, Pearl, and my mother, who passed on her wisdom.

NOT GOOD ENOUGH Inspired by my grandmother, Pearl.

MOP, MOP, MOP For my children, who lovingly and consistently reveal to me my own shortcomings and hypocrisy.

Notes

CHORE CHARTS   Inspired by 2 Nephi 5 and my children.

BAPTIST TESTIMONY and **CRUSHED VELVET**   Inspired by a dear friend in our D2 ward.

MY THOUGHTS ≠ YOUR THOUGHTS – FINDING MOTHER   These poems were written in response to my mother-in-law's sudden illness and passing. We miss you, Karen.

THEY CAME RUNNING   I honestly can't remember if I wrote this before or after I read "Preparations" by Kenneth Bernard (found in *Sudden Fiction International: Sixty Short-Short Stories*, edited by Robert Shapard and James Thomas, New York: Norton, 1989). I do know that my mother-in-law passed away in November 2018 and that I read "Preparations" in January 2019 and that I was writing a lot about death at the time.

BURNT OFFERINGS and **OBJECT PERMANENCE**   So many friends stopped by to offer us meals and treats and condolences when my mother-in-law was dying. I am not a good cook, but I learned that I should keep bringing my offerings because it's not really about the food (though food is often appreciated).

MIRIAM'S WORRY (AND THE ANSWER)   The words Miriam uttered when she learned Grandma wasn't going to get better and the words I was inspired to tell her.

I SEE DEAD PEOPLE   Title borrowed from a very famous line from *The Sixth Sense*.

CHRISTMAS YET TO COME   For Grandpa Frank.

Notes

NANCY HEISS has been writing quietly for years. She received a BA in linguistics from Brigham Young University and is currently pursuing an MA in Literacies and Children's Literature from the University of Georgia. She recently renewed her lease on motherhood with the birth of her sixth child, a welcome surprise. She lives in Georgia with her husband, children, and a cat.

BROOKE NEWHART is a North Carolina-based painter and illustrator. She has a bachelor's degree in fine art from Brigham Young University, and has been detailing scenes of everyday life for the past eight years. She is eager to continue creating. To see more of her work, visit her Instagram @brookenewhart

Made in the USA
Las Vegas, NV
03 February 2022